ALL YOU NEED TO PLAY 16 CHA

Chart Hits

CHORD SONGBOOK
VOLUME 2

International
MUSIC
Publications

International Music Publications Limited
Griffin House 161 Hammersmith Road London W6 8BS England

**DON'T BE
A MUSIC
COPYCAT!**

The copying of © copyright material is a criminal offence and may lead to prosecution.

Series Editors: Sadie Cook and Ulf Klenfe

Music Editorial & Project Management: Artemis Music Lir
Cover photo: Redferns Music Picture Library, A1; Nat Sta
Gary Barlow; Paul Bergen, Robbie Williams; Mick Hutson
Costello; Keith Morris, Westlife; Paul Bergen
Design and production: Space DPS Limited

Published 2000

**International
MUSIC
Publications**

Exclusive Distributors

Carisch

Italy: Via Campania 12
               20098 San Giuliano Milane
               Milano

International Music Publications Limited

England: Griffin House
               161 Hammersmith Road
               London W6 8BS

Spain: Magallanes 25
               28015 Madrid

Germany: Marstallstr. 8
               D-80539 München

France: 20 Rue de la Ville-l'Eveque
               75008 Paris

Denmark: Danmusik
               Vognmagergäde 7
               DK1120 Copenhagen K

Chart Hits

Tablature Key		**4**
Playing Guide		**6**
Beautiful Day	*3 Colours Red*	**7**
Bring It On	*Gomez*	**20**
Burning Down The House	*Tom Jones And The Cardigans*	**10**
Dayz Like That	*Fierce*	**14**
Flying Without Wings	*Westlife*	**23**
In Our Lifetime	*Texas*	**26**
Kiss Me	*Sixpence None The Richer*	**29**
Moving	*Supergrass*	**36**
Music To Watch Girls By	*Andy Williams*	**32**
No Regrets	*Robbie Williams*	**39**
Private Number	*911*	**44**
Rhythm & Blues Alibi	*Gomez*	**47**
Secret Smile	*Semisonic*	**50**
She	*Elvis Costello*	**62**
Stronger	*Gary Barlow*	**54**
Summertime Of Our Lives	*A1*	**58**

Tablature Key

Hammer-on

Play the first note with one finger then 'hammer' another finger on the fret indicated.

Pull-off

Place both fingers on the notes to be sounded, play the first note and, without picking, pull the finger off to sound the lower note.

Gliss

Play the first note and then slide the same fret-hand finger up or down to the second note. Don't strike the second note.

Gliss and restrike

Same as legato slide, except the second note is struck.

Quarter-tone bend

Play the note then bend up a quarter-tone.

Half-tone bend

Play the note then bend up a semi-tone.

Whole-tone bend

Play the note then bend up a whole-tone.

Bend of more than a tone

Play the note then bend up as required.

Bend and return

Play the note, bend up as indicated, then return back to the original note.

Compound bend and return

Play the note then bend up and down in the rhythm shown.

Pre-bend

Bend the note as shown before striking.

Pre-bend and return

Bend the note as shown before striking it, then return it back to its original pitch.

Unison bend

Play the two notes together and bend the lower note up to the pitch of the higher one.

Double stop bend and return

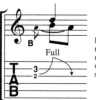

Hold the top note, then bend and return the bottom notes on a lower string.

Bend and restrike

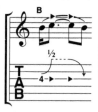

Play the note, bend as shown, then restrike the string where indicated.

Bend and tap

Bend the note as shown and tap the higher fret while still holding the bend.

Vibrato

Rapidly bend and release the note with the fretting hand.

Trill

Rapidly alternate between the notes indicated by continuously hammering on and pulling off.

Tapping

Hammer ('tap') the fret indicated with the pick-hand index or middle finger and pull off the note fretted by the fret-hand.

Pick scrape

The edge of the pick is rubbed along the string, producing a scratchy sound.

Muffled strings

Lay the fret-hand lightly across the strings then play with the pick-hand.

Natural harmonic

Play the note while the fret-hand lightly touches the string directly over the fret indicated.

Pinch harmonic

Fret the note normally and produce a harmonic by adding the edge of the thumb or the tip of the index finger of the pick hand to the normal pick attack.

Harp harmonic

Fret the note normally and gently rest the pick-hand's index finger directly above the indicated fret while the pick-hand's thumb or pick assists by plucking the appropriate string.

Palm muting

Allow the pick-hand to rest lightly on the strings whilst playing.

Rake

Drag the pick across the strings shown with a single motion.

Tremolo picking

Repeatedly pick the note as rapidly as possible.

Arpeggiate

Play the notes of the chord by rolling them in the direction of the arrow.

Vibrato-bar dive and return

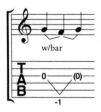

Drop the pitch of the note or chord a specific number of steps (in rhythm) then return to the original pitch.

Vibrato-bar dips

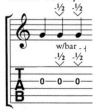

Play the first note then use the bar to drop a specific number of steps, then release back to the original pitch, in rhythm. Only the first note is picked.

Playing Guide

Tuning Your Guitar

To enjoy this book to the full, you have to ensure that your guitar is in tune.

There are many different methods of tuning your guitar. One of the most common is relative tuning. This is how it works.

Tune the low (thick) E-string to a comfortable pitch, fret the string at the 5th fret and then play it together with the A-string. Adjust the A-string until both strings have the same pitch. Repeat this procedure for the rest of the strings as follows:

  5th fret A-string to open D-string
  5th fret D-string to open G-string
  4th fret G-string to open B-string
  5th fret B-string to open E-string

After a little practise, you will be able to do this in a matter of minutes.

Chords and Chord boxes

Chords consist of several notes played together and are the basis for accompanying songs.

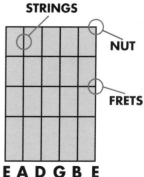

A chord box is simply a diagram showing a portion of the guitar neck. The horizontal lines illustrate the frets (the top line indicates the nut) and the vertical lines illustrate the strings, starting with the thickest string (low E) on the left. A fret number next to the chord box indicates that the chord should be played in that position, higher up on the neck.

The black dots indicate where to place your fingers on the fretboard. An 'O' instructs you to play the string open and an 'X' indicates that the string should not be played.

Basic Playing Techniques

Most guitarists use a pick to strum and pluck the strings. You could use your fingers, but they tend to wear out more quickly than a pick! There are no rules as to how to hold a pick - if it's comfortable, it's right for you.

You can use upstrokes, downstrokes or both. The most common is a combination of the two, alternating up and downstrokes. Ensure that you maintain an even, steady tempo when you strum your chords.

Most importantly... have fun!

Beautiful Day

Words and Music by
PETER VUCKOVIC

Fm(add4) E♭sus4 D♭6(no3) A♭sus2 D♭5 D♭maj7(no3) Fm11 E♭

D♭sus2 D♭ A♭/D♭ G♭5 B♭5 Fsus4 Fm A♭5

♩ = 64   *Tune guitar down one semitone*

Verse 1 $\frac{4}{4}$ Fm^{add4} | E♭^{sus4} |

Things you forget to say   will haunt

D♭6(no3) | Fm^{add4} |

you.   Been down here a million days.

E♭sus4 | A♭sus2 |

I know you'll   get   me   through

Fm^{add4} | E♭sus4 |

You don't need to stay   because I'll

D♭6(no3) | Fm^{7add4} |

never been alone.   Do you cry

E♭ | D♭sus2 |

a - nymore?

D♭ |

No more.

Chorus 1   A♭^{sus2} | E♭ |

You're in the never ending,   bitter and condescending. Blue,

G♭5 | B♭5   F^{sus4} |

I   just   wanna be by you.

A♭sus2 | E♭   E♭sus4 E♭ |

And everything will turn to blue, the dream is a fallacy come true.

G♭5 | **B♭5**   **Fsus4** |
I just wanna spend some time with you

A♭sus2 | **Fm7add4** |
on a beautiful day.

     E♭   **D♭sus2**
| /   /   /   / | /   /   /   / |

Verse 2   **Fmadd4** | **E♭sus4** |
Seein' the mornin' in,   forget

D♭6(no3) | **Fmadd4** |
to   worry about the things

E♭sus4 | **A♭sus2** |
that hurt you.

Fmadd4 | **E♭sus4** |
You're becoming dependent now,   is it

D♭6(no3) | **Fm7add4** |
cold where you are too?

E♭ | **D♭sus2** |
Freeze   no   more,

D♭ |
No more.

Chorus 2   **A♭sus2** | **E♭** |
You're in the never ending,   bitter and condescending. Blue,

G♭5 | **B♭5**   **Fsus4** |
I   just   wanna   be by you.

A♭sus2 | **E♭**   **E♭sus4 E♭** |
And everything will turn to blue, the dream is a fallacy come true.

G♭5 | **B♭5**   **Fsus4** |
I just wanna spend some time with you

A♭sus2   **|Fm⁷ᵃᵈᵈ⁴**   **|**

on a beautiful day.

E♭   **|D♭sus2**   **|**

We got it so throw it away,

Verse 3 **Fm⁷ᵃᵈᵈ⁴**   **|E♭**   **|**

'cos we will be as luck-y as the last time, child.

D♭   **|Fm⁷ᵃᵈᵈ⁴**   **|**

The habits don't blow it away,   now we are on the oth-

E♭   **|D♭**   **|**

er side. And you know you're talking 'bout the old times,

E♭   **| $\frac{2}{4}$ Fm** **A♭5** **|**

walking down an open road but failing to dis-

$\frac{4}{4}$ D♭5   **D♭**   **|E♭**   **|**

guise,   revealing the signs.

    A♭sus2   **E♭**

| / / / / **|** / / / / **|**

G♭5   **|A♭sus2**   **|**

Nothing you can do will change me.   It's a beautiful

Fm⁷ᵃᵈᵈ⁴   **|E♭**   **|**

day.   Ooh,

D♭   **|A♭sus2**   **‖**

ooh,   oh.

Burning Down The House

Words and Music by
DAVID BYRNE, TINA WEYMOUTH, CHRIS FRANTZ AND JERRY HARRISON

F#7   B7   E   B7/E

F#   G#   B7/F#

♩ = 108

Intro   F#7   N.C.

4/4 | / / / / | / / / / |

| B7 |

Fighting fire with fire.

Verse 1   F#7 |E |

Watch   out.   You might get walked on after

F#7 |E   B7/E |

cool   baby's   strange but not a stranger.

F#7 |E |

I'm an ordinary   guy.

F#   G# |N.C.   B7/E |

Burning down the house.

Verse 2   F#7 |E |

Hold   tight.   Wait till the party's over

F#7 |E   B7/E |

Hold   tight.   We're in for nasty weather

F#7 |E |

There has got to be a way.

F#   G# | N.C. |
     Burning down the house.

Chorus 1 $F\sharp^7$ | E |
    Here's your ticket. Pack your bag. It's time for jumping overboard.

    $F\sharp^7$ | E B^7/E |
     The transportation is here.

    $F\sharp^7$ | E |
    Close enough but not too far. Maybe you know where you are.

    F# | E B^7 |
     Fighting fire with fire.

Verse 3 $F\sharp^7$ | E |
     All wet.   Yeah, you might need a raincoat.

    $F\sharp^7$ | E B^7/E |
     Shake down. Dreams walking in broad daylight.

    $F\sharp^7$ | E |
     Three hundred and sixty-five degrees.

    F#   G# | N.C. |
     Burning down the house.

Chorus 2 $F\sharp^7$ | E |
    It was once upon a place. Some-times I listen to myself.

    $F\sharp^7$ | E B^7/E |
     Going or coming first place.

    $F\sharp^7$ | E |
    People on their way to way to work, baby did you expect.

    F# | E B^7 |
     I'm gonna burst into flames.

    F# | E |
     Fighting fire with fire.

| **F#7** | /   /   /   / | **E**   /   /   **B7/E**   /   / |

F# | **E** |
Fighting fire with fire.

F#   **G#** | **2/4**   **B7** |
Burning down the house.

Verse 4   **4/4 F#7** | **E** |
My   house.   S'out of the ordinary,

F#7 | **E**   **B7/E** |
That's   right.   Don't wanna hurt nobody.

F#7 | **E** |
Some   things   sure   can   sweep me off   my feet.

F#   **G#** | **2/4**   **B7/E** |
Burning down the house.

Verse 5   **4/4 F#7** | **E** |
Watch   out.   You might get what you're after,

F#7 | **E**   **B7/E** |
cool   baby's   strange but not a stranger.

F#7 | **E** |
I'm an ordinary   guy.

F#   **G#** |
Burning down the house.

F#7 | **E** |
Three hundred and sixty-five   degrees.

F#   **G#** | **N.C.** |
Burning down the house.   Fighting fire with

F#   **G#** | **N.C.** |
fire.   Fighting fire with fire.   Gonna burst into

F#   **G#**   **| N.C.** |
flames.   Fighting fire with fire.   Fighting fire with

F#   **G#**   **| N.C.** |
fire.   Fighting fire with fire.   Gonna burst into

F#   **G#**   **| N.C.** |
flames.   *Burning down the house.*   My   house.

F#   **G#**   **| N.C.** |
           Burning down the house.   No

F#   **G#**   **| N.C.** |
visible means of support and   you have not seen nothing yet but

F#   **G#**   **| N.C.** | .
         ev'rything's stuck toge-ther.

F#7   **| E** |
I don't know what you expect star-ing into your T.V. set

F#7   **| E**   **B7/F#** |
     Fighting fire with fire.

Coda   **F#7**   **E**
| /   /   /   / | /   /   /   / |

F#   **| E**   **B7/F#** |
Ooh   burning down the house.

(Repeat Coda to fade)

Dayz Like That

Words and Music by
ALISTAIR TENNANT, K-GEE AND MICHELLE ESCOFFERY

$\downarrow$ = 110

Intro

$C\sharp m^{11}$ | $C\sharp m^7$ $G\sharp m^7$ | $F\sharp m^7$ |

$C\sharp m^7$ $G\sharp m^7$ | $F\sharp m^7$ |

Yea,   yea,   baby.

Verse 1

$C\sharp m^7$ $G\sharp m^7$

Now that you think about it,

$F\sharp m^7$

how do you feel about it?

$C\sharp m^7$ $G\sharp m^7$

You've had some time to live with   the mes-

$F\sharp m^7$

ses   that you made.

$C\sharp m^7$ $G\sharp m^7$

Not trying to say I'm perfect.

$F\sharp m^7$

Push comes to shove I'm worth it.

$C\sharp m^7$ $G\sharp m^7$

There were things you've had to deal with,   but it's al-

$F\sharp m^7$

right   'cause we're still tied,   yea, yea.   I

C♯m⁷   **G♯m⁷** |
can't believe you're back again after all you put me through.

F♯m⁷ |
Even though I'm still your friend I don't want to be with you. Re-

Chorus 1

C♯m⁷   **G♯m⁷** |
member when days   were like that,   I was loving

F♯m⁷ |
you every time   you loved back,   and now you're

C♯m⁷   **G♯m⁷** |
telling me that   you miss that,   bet you feel lone-

F♯m⁷ |
ly   but it's like that.   Do you re-

C♯m⁷   **G♯m⁷** |
member when days   were like that,   I was loving

F♯m⁷ |
you every time   you loved back,   and now you're

C♯m⁷   **G♯m⁷** |
telling me that   you miss that,   bet you feel lone-

F♯m⁷ |
ly   that you lost me baby.

Verse 2

C♯m⁷   **G♯m⁷** |
Now that I think about it,

F♯m⁷ |
there were some things I regret.

C♯m⁷   **G♯m⁷** |
I should have never just let   you walk

F♯m⁷ |
away and not explain.

C#m⁷   G#m⁷ |

But I'm a   it   no, no,

F#m⁷

I had to get over it.

C#m⁷   G#m⁷

It made me stronger within.   There's a les-

F#m⁷

son here,   hope you learn from it,   ooh, yea. I

C#m⁷   G#m⁷

can't believe you're back again after all you put me through.

F#m⁷

Even though I'm still your friend I don't want to be with you. Re-

Chorus 2   C#m⁷   G#m⁷

member when days   were like that,   I was loving

F#m⁷

you every time   you loved back,   and now you're

C#m⁷   G#m⁷

telling me that   you miss that,   bet you feel lone-

F#m⁷

ly   but it's like that.   Do you re-

C#m⁷   G#m⁷

member when days   were like that,   I was loving

F#m⁷

you every time   you loved back,   and now you're

C#m⁷   G#m⁷

telling me that   you miss that,   bet you feel lone-

F#m⁷

ly   that you lost me baby.

C#m⁷   G#m⁷ |F#m⁷

yea.

$C^{\sharp}m^7$ $G^{\sharp}m^7$ $F^{\sharp}m^7$

| / / / / | / / / / |

Bridge

$F^{\sharp}m^7$ |
We can be friends   but not lovers,

$C^{\sharp}m^7$ |
ah, ooh,   ooh,   ooh,   oh,   oh,

$F^{\sharp}m^7$ |
got to be one   not the other,

$C^{\sharp}m^7$ |
         better understand I'm not playing.

$F^{\sharp}m^7$ |
We can be friends   but not lovers,

$C^{\sharp}m^7$ |
ah, ooh,   ooh,   ooh,   oh,   oh,

$F^{\sharp}m^7$ |
got to be one   not the other,

$C^{\sharp}m^7$ |
         better understand I'm not playing,

|
playing,   playing.   Do you re-

Chorus 3

$C^{\sharp}m^7$ $G^{\sharp}m^7$ |
member when days   were like that,   I was loving

$F^{\sharp}m^7$ |
you every time   you loved back,   and now you're

$C^{\sharp}m^7$ $G^{\sharp}m^7$ |
telling me that   you miss that,   bet you feel lone-

$F^{\sharp}m^7$ |
ly   but it's like that.   Do you re-

C#m⁷   **G#m⁷** |
member when days   were like that,   I was loving

F#m⁷ |
you every time   you loved back,   and now you're

C#m⁷   **G#m⁷** |
telling me that   you miss that,   bet you feel lone-

F#m⁷ |
ly   that you lost me.   Do you re-

C#m⁷   **G#m⁷** |
member when days   were like that,   I was loving

F#m⁷ |
you every time   you loved back,   and now you're

C#m⁷   **G#m⁷** |
telling me that   you miss that,   bet you feel lone-

F#m⁷ |
ly   but it's like that.   Do you re-

C#m⁷   **G#m⁷** |
member when days   were like that,   I was loving

F#m⁷ |
you every time   you loved back,   and now you're

C#m⁷   **G#m⁷** |
telling me that   you miss that,   bet you feel lone-

F#m⁷ |
ly   that you lost me baby.

      C#m⁷   **G#m⁷**   **F#m⁷**
| /   /   /   / | /   /   /   / |

C#m⁷   **G#m⁷** | **F#m⁷** |
            Yea,   yea,   baby.

      C#m⁷   **G#m⁷**   **F#m⁷**
| /   /   /   / | /   /   /   / |

$C\sharp m^7$ $G\sharp m^7$ |$F\sharp m^7$ |
        Yea, yea.   Do you re-

Chorus 4 $C\sharp m^7$ $G\sharp m^7$ |
      member when days were like that,   I was loving

$F\sharp m^7$ |
you every time   you loved back,   and now you're

$C\sharp m^7$ $G\sharp m^7$ |
telling me that   you miss that,   bet you feel lone-

$F\sharp m^7$ |
ly   but it's like that.   Do you re-

$C\sharp m^7$ $G\sharp m^7$ |
member when days were like that,   I was loving

$F\sharp m^7$ |
you every time   you loved back,   and now you're

$C\sharp m^7$ $G\sharp m^7$ |
telling me that   you miss that,   bet you feel lone-

$F\sharp m^7$ |
ly   that you lost me. I   bet   you   feel

                    ‖

lonely.

Bring It On

Words and Music by
PAUL BLACKBURN, THOMAS WILLIAM GRAY, OLIVER JAMES PEACOCK,
IAN THOMAS BALL AND BENJAMIN JOSEPH OTTEWELL

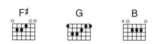

Verse 2

F# | | | |
If I lied and told you that you're dif-ficult   or hard to take   I'd

G | |F# | |
lie.   I'd   still lie.

F# | | | |
If you try to please me now, you know that I won't remonstrate, but

G | |F# | |
lie.   I'd   still lie.

Chorus 2

F# |B |F# |B |
Bring it on. Make   it right.   Bring it on. To   the light.

F# |B |F# |B |
Pick me up   sa-tellite.   If it's wrong make   it right.

Interlude

N.C.

| / / / / | / / / / | / / / / | / / / / |

| / / / / | / / / / | / / / / | / / / / |

   F#   B   F#   B

| / / / / | / / / / | / / / / | / / / / |

   F#   B   F#   B

| / / / / | / / / / | / / / / | / / / / |

Bridge

F# |B |F# |B |
We   like   quiet   nights   on   the

F# |B |F# |B |
island.   Ah   ah   ah   ah.

F# |B |F# |B |
We   have   battered stars   round our heads.

| F# | B | F# | B |
| | | Ah   ah   ah   ah. |

F# |B |F# |B |
We   can   reach new heights in this

F# |B |F# |B |
silence.   Ah   ah   ah   ah.

F# |B |F# |B |
We're   dragged slowly   to-wards the end.

F# |B |F# |B |
                          Ah   ah   ah   ah.

Chorus 2   F# |B |F# |B |
Bring it on. Make   it right.   Bring it on. To   the light.

F# |B |F# |B |
Pick me up   sa-tellite.   If it's wrong make   it right.

F# |B |F# |B |
Bring it on. Make   it right.   Bring it on. To   the light.

F# |B |F# |B |
Pick me up   sa-tellite.   If it's wrong make   it right.

Coda   F#

| / / / / | / / / / | / / / / | / / / / |

| / / / / | / / / / | / / / / | / / / / |

           | | ‖
If I was   inor-dinately   dif-ferent .

Flying Without Wings

Words and Music by
STEVE MAC AND WAYNE HECTOR

A♭add9	Fm11	D♭add9	E♭	D♭	A♭	E♭/G

F♯m7	D♭m	E♭11	D♭/A♭	D♭/F	E♭/D♭	Dm7(♭5)

♩ = 72

Verse 1   4/4 N.C. | A♭add9 | |

Ev'rybody's looking for that something.   One thing that makes it all

Fm11 | |

complete.   You find it in the strangest

D♭add9 | |

places.   Places you never knew it

E♭ | |

could be.   Some find it in the face of

A♭add9 | |

their children.   Some find it in their lov-

Fm11 | |

er's eyes.   Who can deny the joy it

D♭ | E♭ |

brings when you've found the special thing. You're flying without

A♭add9 | |

wings.   Some find it sharing ev'ry

Verse 2   **A♭add9** | |

morning,   some in their solita-

Fm11 | |

ry lives.   You find it in the words of

© 1999 & 2000 Rondor Music (London) Ltd, London SW6 4TW and Rokstone Music, London
SW6 4TA

D♭add9
others. | | A simple line can make you

E♭
laugh or cry. | | You find it in the deepest

A♭add9
friendship. | | The girl you cherish all

Fm^{11}
life. | | And when you know how much that

D♭ | **E♭** |
means, you've found that special thing. You're flying without

E♭
wings. | | So impossi-

Bridge
D♭ | **E♭** |
ble as they may seem, you've got to

Fm^7　　**E♭/G** | **A♭**　　**E♭/G** |
fight　for every　dream.　'Cause who's to

D♭add9 | **D♭m** |
know　which one you let go　will have made you com-

E♭^{11}　**E♭** | **E♭^{11}**　**E♭** |
plete.　With　me it's　waking up be-

Coda
A♭　**D♭/A♭** | **A♭**　**E♭/G** |
side you,　to watch the sun rise on your

Fm^7　**D♭/F** | **Fm^7** |
face.　To know that I can say I

D♭　**E♭/D♭** | **D♭** |
love you,　at any given time or

E♭　**A♭/E♭** | **E♭^{7}** |
place.　It's little things that only

A♭   D♭/A♭ | A♭   E♭/G |
I know,   those are the things that make

F♭m⁷ → Fm⁷   D♭/F | Fm⁷ |
you mine.   And it's like flying without

Fm⁷   **D♭/F**   **| Fm⁷**   **|**
you mine.   And it's like flying without

D♭   **| D♭**   **|**
wings,   'cause you're my special thing.   I'm flying without

E♭   **A♭/E♭**   **| E♭⁷**   **|**
wings.   And you're the place my life begins

D♭   **| E♭**   **|**
and you'll be where it ends,   I'm flying without

D♭   **Dm⁷⁽♭⁵⁾**   **| E♭¹¹**   **|**
wings. And that's the joy   you bring.   I'm flying without

D♭   **‖**
wings.

In Our Lifetime

Words and Music by
JOHN McELHONE AND SHARLEEN SPITERI

Chord diagrams: E6 · Eadd9 · Amaj7 · A6 · B6 · B · C#m · C#sus2 · A

Chord diagrams: G#m · E · F#m7 · F#m9 · F#m · Asus2 · Badd9 · Bsus2¼

♩ = 94

Intro $\frac{4}{4}$ **E⁶**   **Eadd⁹** | |

Ah ah ah

Amaj7   **A⁶**   **B⁶**   **B**

| / / / / | / / / / |

Verse 1   **C♯m**   **C♯sus2** | |
There are things   I can't tell you,

A | |
I love you too much to say.

C♯m   **C♯sus2** | |
I stand undressed, but   I'm not naked,

A | |
you look at me and who I   am.   Understand

G♯m | |
that it is hard to tell you that I've given all   I

A | |
have to give.   And I can un-

G♯m | |
derstand your feelings, but then ev-erybody has   a

A |B |
life to live.   Once in a

© 1999 EMI 10 Music Ltd, London WC2H 0EA

Chorus 1

E   E$^{\text{add9}}$ | E   E$^{\text{add9}}$ |
lifetime,   you have what I've seen,

A$^{\text{maj7}}$ A^6 | A$^{\text{maj7}}$ A^6 |
you will always swim for shore.   Once in my

F$^\sharp$m^7 F$^\sharp$m^9 F$^\sharp$m | A$^{\text{maj7}}$ A^6 |
life - time,   I'll never be in between,

B^6 B | B^6 B |
some things you just can't ignore.

Verse 2

C$^\sharp$m   C$^\sharp$sus2 | |
Now reach out,   you can touch me,

A | |
I'll let you have my life to share.

C$^\sharp$m   C$^\sharp$sus2 | |
The years, the days   and the minutes,

A | |
yeah,time has such a puzzling grace. Understand

G$^\sharp$m | |
that it is hard to tell you that I've given all   I

A | |
have to give.   And I can un-

G$^\sharp$m | |
derstand your feelings, but then everybody has   a

A | B |
life to live.   Once in a

Chorus 2

E   E$^{\text{add9}}$ | E   E$^{\text{add9}}$ |
lifetime,   you have what I've seen,

A$^{\text{maj7}}$ A^6 | A$^{\text{maj7}}$ A^6 |
you will always swim for shore.   Once in my

F#m⁷ F#m⁹ F#m |Amaj7   A⁶ |
life - time,   I'll never be in between,

B⁶   B |B⁶   B |
some things you just can't ignore.   Once in a

E   Eadd9 |E   Eadd9 |
lifetime,   you have what I've seen,

Amaj7   A⁶ |Amaj7   A⁶ |
you will always swim for shore.   Once in my

F#m⁷ F#m⁹ F#m |Amaj7   A⁶ |
life - time,   I'll never be in between,

B⁶   B |B⁶   B |
some things you just can't ignore.   I just need

Interlude   E⁶ E   E⁶ |E⁶   E   E⁶   Eadd9 |
to   have your   love, I just   can't say no.   It's a gift

A   Asus2   A |A   Asus2   A |
from   way   above, I just   can't say no.   It's the one

Badd9   B   Badd9 |Badd9 B   Bsus |
big   difference. If there's one thing I can't have, I just

E⁶   E   E⁶ |E   Eadd9 |
can't say no,   I just can't say no. *(Hey, hey, hey)* Once in a

Chorus 3   E   Eadd9 |E   Eadd9 |
lifetime,   you have what I've seen,

Amaj7   A⁶ |Amaj7   A⁶ |
you will always swim for shore.   Once in my

F#m⁷ F#m⁹ F#m |Amaj7   A⁶ |
life - time,   I'll never be in between,

B⁶   B |B⁶   B |
some things you just can't ignore.   Once in a

(Repeat Chorus to fade)

Kiss Me

Words and Music by
MATT SLOCUM

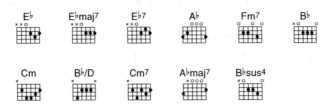

♩ = 100   Capo at 1st fret

Intro

| Eb | | | | Ebmaj7 | | | | Eb7 | | | | Ebmaj7 | | | |
$\frac{4}{4}$ | / / / / | / / / / | / / / / | / / / / |

| Eb | | | | Ebmaj7 | | | | Eb7 | | | | Ebmaj7 | | | |
| / / / / | / / / / | / / / / | / / / / |

Verse 1

Eb |Ebmaj7

Kiss me,   out of the bearded barley

Eb7 |Ebmaj7

nightly,   beside the green, green grass,

Eb |Ebmaj7

swing, swing,   swing the spinning step,

Eb7 |Ab

you wear those shoes and I will   wear that dress,   oh,

Chorus 1

Fm7   Bb |Eb   Cm

kiss me   beneath the milky twilight,

Fm7   Bb |Eb   Eb7

lead me   out on the moonlit floor,

Fm7   Bb |Eb   Cm

lift your   open hand   strike up the band   and make the fire-

Cm⁷   **Eb**   **| Ab maj7** |

flies dance, silver moon's sparkling.

Bb sus4   **Bb**   **| Eb** |

              So kiss me.

     Eb maj7   **Eb 7**   **Eb maj7**

| / / / / | / / / / | / / / / |

Verse 2   **Eb**   **| Eb maj7** |

          Kiss me,   down by the broken treehouse,

Eb 7   **| Eb maj7** |

          swing   me,   upon its hanging tire,

Eb   **| Eb maj7** |

          bring, bring,   bring your flowered hat,

Eb 7   **| Ab** |

    we'll take the trail marked on your father's map,   oh

Chorus 2   **Fm⁷**   **Bb**   **| Eb**   **Cm** |

        kiss me   beneath the milky twilight,

Fm⁷   **Bb**   **| Eb**   **Eb 7** |

      lead me   out on the moonlit floor,

Fm⁷   **Bb**   **| Eb**   **Cm** |

lift your   open hand   strike up the band and make the fire-

Cm⁷   **Eb**   **| Ab maj7** |

flies dance, silver moon's sparkling.

Bb sus4   **Bb**   **| Eb** |

          So kiss me.

     Eb maj7   **Eb 7**   **Eb maj7**

| / / / / | / / / / | / / / / |

    Fm⁷ **Bb**   **Eb**   **Cm**   **Fm⁷** **Bb**   **Eb**   **Eb 7**

| / / / / | / / / / | / / / / | / / / / |

Chorus 3

```
Fm7              Bb            | Eb                      Cm     |
     kiss me                       beneath the milky twilight,

Fm7              Bb            | Eb                   Eb7       |
     lead me                          out on the moonlit floor,

Fm7           Bb           | Eb                 Cm              |
lift your     open hand      strike up the band  and make the fire-

Cm7              Eb            | Abmaj7                         |
flies dance, silver moon's sparkling.

Bbsus4           Bb            | Eb                             |
                          So kiss  me.

   Ebmaj7        Eb7           Ebmaj7
| / / / /      | / / / /     | / / / /     |

   Eb            Ebmaj7        Eb7           Ebmaj7
| / / / /      | / / / /     | / / / /     | / / / /     |

   Ebmaj7        Eb
| / / / /      | / / / /     ||
```

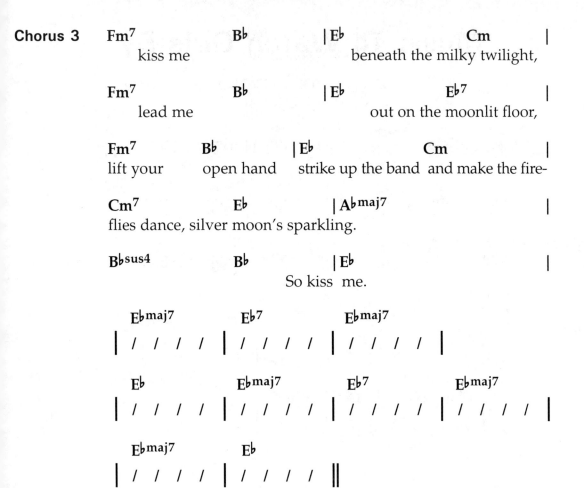

Music To Watch Girls By

Words by TONY VERONA
Music by SID RAMIN

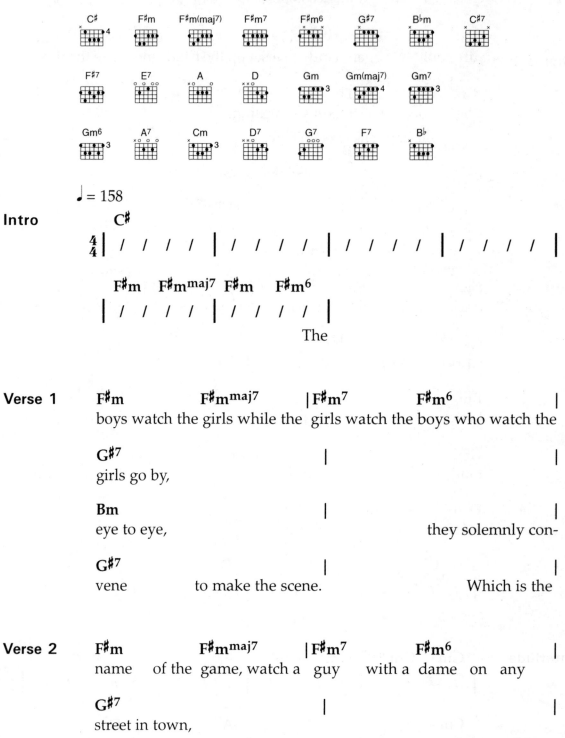

♩ = 158

Intro   C#

4/4 | / / / / | / / / / | / / / / | / / / / |

F#m   F#m^maj7   F#m   F#m^6

| / / / / | / / / / |

The

Verse 1   F#m   F#m^maj7 |F#m^7   F#m^6 |

boys watch the girls while the girls watch the boys who watch the

G#7 | |

girls go by,

Bm | |

eye to eye,   they solemnly con-

G#7 | |

vene   to make the scene.   Which is the

Verse 2   F#m   F#m^maj7 |F#m^7   F#m^6 |

name   of the game, watch a guy   with a dame on any

G#7 | |

street in town,

Bm | |
up and down, and over and a-

G#7 | |
cross, romance is boss.

Chorus 1 **F#7** |**Bm** |
Guys   talk.   Girls   talk.

E7 |**A** |
It happens everywhere.

C#7 |**F#m** |
Eyes   watch,   girls   walk

G#7 |**C#7** | |
with tender loving care.   It's keeping

F#m   **F#m^maj7** |**F#m7**   **F#m6** |
track   of the pack watching   them watching back that makes the

G#7 | |
world go round.

Bm | |
Watch that sound   each time you hear a

G#7 |**C#7** |
loud   collective sigh   they're making

F#m   **Bm**   **F#m** |
music   to watch girls by.

        C#   **D**
| / / / / | / / / / | / / / / | / / / / |

Interlude   **Gm**   **Gm^maj7** **Gm7**   **Gm6**   **A7**
| / / / / | / / / / | / / / / | / / / / |

        Cm   **A7**   **D7**
| / / / / | / / / / | / / / / | / / / / |

| Gm   Gm^maj7 Gm^7   Gm^6   A^7
| / / / / | / / / / | / / / / | / / / / |

| Cm   A^7   D^7
| / / / / | / / / / | / / / / | / / / / |

Chorus 2   G^7 |Cm |
         Guys   talk.   Girls   talk.

         F^7 |B♭ |
                  It happens everywhere.

         D^7 |Gm |
         Eyes   watch,   girls   walk

         A^7 |D^7 | |
                  with tender loving care.   It's keeping

Gm   Gm^maj7 |Gm^7   Gm^6 |
track   of the pack watching   them watching back that makes the

A^7 | |
world go round.

Cm | |
Watch that sound   each time you hear a

A^7 |D^7 |
loud   collective sigh   they're making

Gm   Cm   Gm |
music   to watch girls by.

| / / / / | / / / / | / / / / | / / / / |
                                                            The

Verse 3   Gm   Gm^maj7 |Gm^7   Gm^6 |
         boys watch the girls while the girls watch the boys who watch the

         A^7 | |
         girls go by,

34

Cm | |
eye to eye, they solemnly con-

A⁷ |**D⁷** |
vene to make the scene. La la la

Verse 4 **Gm** **Gm^{maj7}** |**Gm⁷** **Gm⁶** |
la la la la la la la la la la la la la

A⁷ | |
la la la

Cm | |
la la la la la la la la

A⁷ |**D⁷** |
la la la la la. La la la

(Repeat Verse to fade)

Moving

Words and Music by
DANIEL GOFFEY, GARETH COOMBES, MICHAEL QUINN AND ROBERT COOMBES

D13sus4   Em(add9)   Csus2   Cadd9   Am7   B7sus2/F#

B7/F#   Bm   A   Em   B7sus2   B7

♩ = 110

Verse 1
$\frac{4}{4}$ **D¹³ˢᵘˢ⁴** | | | |
Moving, just keep moving   till I don't know

Emᵃᵈᵈ⁹ | | | |
why to stay.

Cˢᵘˢ² |**C**ᵃᵈᵈ⁹ |**Am**⁷ | |
I've been moving so long   the   days all feel the

B⁷ˢᵘˢ²**/F♯** | |**B**⁷**/F♯** | |
same.

Verse 2
D¹³ˢᵘˢ⁴ | | | |
Moving, just keep moving,   well I don't know

Emᵃᵈᵈ⁹ | | | |
why to stay.

Cˢᵘˢ² |**C**ᵃᵈᵈ⁹ |**Am**⁷ | |
And no ties to bind me,   no reasons to re-

B⁷ˢᵘˢ²**/F♯** | |**B**⁷**/F♯** |**N.C.**
main.   I've got a

Chorus 1
Bm   **A** |**Em** |
low, low, feeling around   me   and a

Bm   **A** |**Em** |
stone cold feeling inside.   And I just

Bm   **A**   **|Em** |
can't stop messing my mind up   and wasting my

Bm   **A**   **|Em** |
time.   Ooh.   There's a

Bm   **A**   **|Em** |
low, low feeling around   me   and a

Bm   **A**   **|Em** |
stone cold feeling inside.   I've got to

Bm   **A**   **|Em** |
find somebody to help me,   I'll keep you in

B^{7sus2}   **|B^7** |
mind.   So I'll keep

Verse 3   **D^{13sus4}** | | | |
Moving, just keep moving,   well I don't know

Em^{add9} | | | |
who I am.

C^{sus2}   **|C^{add9}**   **|Am^7** | |
    No lead to follow,   there's no way back a-

B^{7sus2}/F$^{\sharp}$ | **|B^7/F$^{\sharp}$** | |
gain.

Verse 4   **D^{13sus4}** | | | |
Moving, keep on moving,   well I feel I'm

Em^{add9} | | | |
born again.

C^{sus2}   **|C^{add9}**   **|Am^7** | |
    And when it's over,   I'll see   you   a-

B^{7sus2}/F$^{\sharp}$ | | | |
gain.

$B^7/F\sharp$ N.C.

| / / / / | / / / / |

Coda D^{13sus4}

| / / / / | / / / / | / / / / | / / / / |

Em^{add9}

| / / / / | / / / / | / / / / | / / / / |

C^{sus2} C^{add9} Am^7

| / / / / | / / / / | / / / / | / / / / |

$B^{7sus2}/F\sharp$ $B^7/F\sharp$ *(repeat Coda to fade)*

| / / / / | / / / / | / / / / | / / / / |

No Regrets

Words and Music by
ROBERT WILLIAMS AND GUY CHAMBERS

♩ = 104   Capo at 3rd fret

Intro

$A\flat maj^9/C$ Cm^7 ... $A\flat maj^9/C$ Cm^7

4/4 | / / / / | / / / / |

$B\flat sus^4$ $B\flat$ $B\flat sus^4$ $B\flat$

| / / / / | / / / / |

$A\flat maj^9/C$ Cm^7 $A\flat maj^9/C$ Cm^7

| / / / / | / / / / |

$B\flat sus^4$ $B\flat$ $B\flat sus^4$ $B\flat$

| / / / / | / / / / |

Verse 1 Cm^7

Tell me a sto-ry

$B\flat sus^4$ $B\flat$

where we all changed,

Cm^7

and we 'd live our lives   together

$B\flat sus^4$ $B\flat$

and not estranged.

Gm |G

I didn't lose   my mind,   it was

Fm^7 |A$\flat$maj7 |
mine   to give away.

Gm |G |
    Couldn't stay to watch   me cry,   you didn't

Fm^7 |B$\flat$ |
have the time.   So I softly   slip away.

| /   /   /   / |

Chorus 1   Fm^9 | |
                            No regrets.

Cm^7 | |
                    They don't work.

Fm^9 | |
                    No regrets   now.

B$\flat$ | |
                They only hurt.

Fm^9 | |
                Sing me a love   song.

Cm^7 | |
                Drop me a line.

Dm$^{7(\flat 5)}$ | |
                Suppose it's   just   a point   of view

G | |
                but they tell me I'm   doing   fine.

Interlude   Cm^7 B$\flat$sus4 B$\flat$ B$\flat$sus4 B$\flat$
| / / / / | / / / / | / / / / | / / / / |

Cm^7 B$\flat$sus4 B$\flat$ B$\flat$sus4 B$\flat$
| / / / / | / / / / | / / / / | / / / / |

Verse 2   **Cm⁷** | |

                      I know from the out-side

B♭sus4 **B♭** | |

           we look good for each oth-er.

Cm⁷ | |

               Felt things were go-ing   wrong   when

B♭sus4 **B♭** | |

           you didn't like my moth-er.

Gm |**G** |

              I don't want   to hate   but that's

Fm⁷ |**A♭maj7** |

all   you've left   me with.

Gm |**G** |

              A bitter af-tertaste   and a fan-

Fm⁷ |**B♭** |

tasy   of how   we all   could live.

     | /   /   /   / |

Chorus 2   **Fm⁹** | |

               No regrets.

Cm⁷ | |

           They don't work.

Fm⁹ | |

              No regrets   now.

B♭ | |

           They only hurt.

Fm⁹ | |

     I know they're still talk-ing,

Cm⁷ | |

       the demons in your head.

Dm$^{7(\flat 5)}$ | |
If I could just stop hating you

G | |
I feel sorry   for us   in-

Bridge **A$\flat$** | |
stead.   Remember the pho-tographs?   *Insane.*

F/A | |
The ones where we all laughed.   *How lame.*

A$\flat$ | |
We were having the time of our lives.   Well thank-

F/A |G^{7}/B |
you,   it was a real   blast.

G$^{\text{aug5}}$
| /   /   /   / |

Chorus 3 **Fm^{9}** | |
No regrets.

Cm^{7} | |
They don't work.

Fm^{9} | |
No regrets   now.

B$\flat$ | |
They only hurt.

Fm^{9} | |
Sing me a love   song.

Cm^{7} | |
Drop me a line.

Dm$^{7(\flat 5)}$ | |
Suppose it's   just   a point   of view

G | |

but they tell me I'm doing fine.

Interlude

Cm   **D⁷/C**

| / / / / | / / / / | / / / / | / / / / |

Cm   **D⁷/C**

| / / / / | / / / / | / / / / | / / / / |

Coda

Cm | |

Spoken Everything I wanted to be, everytime I walked away,

D | **G⁷**

every time you told me to leave I just wanted to stay.

Cm |

Every time you looked at me and every time you smiled

D | **G⁷**

I felt so vacant. You treat me like a child.

Cm |

I loved the way we used to laugh, I loved the way we used to smile.

D | **G⁷**

Often I sit down and think of you for a while.

Cm |

And then it passes me by and I think of someone else in-

D | **G⁷**

stead. I guess the love we once had is officially

‖

dead.

Private Number

Words and Music by
BOOKER JONES AND WILLIAM BELL

C#m   B   A   G#m7/B   E   F#   Gm   C#   D

Dadd9   A/B   A6   F#m   F#7   F#m7   Bsus4   E/G#

♩ = 102

Intro   C#m   B   A   C#m   G#m7/B   A

| / / / / | / / / / | / / / / | / / / / |

Yeah, yeah, yeah.

Verse 1   E |B   A |

(Male) Since I've been gone   you've had your

E |B   A |
number changed.   Mm, yeah.

E |B   A |
      But my love for you,   girl,   still re-

E |B   A |
mains the same.   Mm.   Now

A   F# |B |
I've been lovin' you,   and

Gm |C# |
you've been lovin' me   so

D |Dadd9 |
long,   baby what's

A/B | B |
wrong?   So I'm asking,

Chorus 1   E |A6 |
baby,   baby,   ba-by,

F#m   B |E |
please   let me have your num-ber,   yeah.

|A⁶ |
Baby, baby, ba - by,

F♯m B |E |
please let me have your num-ber, yeah.

Verse 2

E |B A |
(Female) I'm sorry you couldn't call me when

E |B A |
you got home. Well I tried to call you baby

E |B A |
But other fellas kept on calling while

E |B A |
you were gone. So

A F♯ |B |
I had my number changed, but

Gm |C♯ |
I'm not acting strange. Welcome

D |Dadd9 |
home, baby nothin's

A/B | B |
wrong. So I'm asking,

Chorus 2

E |A⁶ |
baby, baby, ba - by,

F♯m B |E |
you can have my private num-ber,

|A⁶ |
Baby, baby, ba - by,

F♯m B |E |
you can have my private num-ber,

Verse 3

E |B A |
(Male) So if I call you, will you be home?

E |B A |
(Female) *I will be waiting there by the phone.* (Male) Now

          E   **|B**   **A**   **|**
(Both) I know your number,   though it's been changed.

E   **|B**   **A**   **|**
Tell me now baby,   love still remains.

A   **F#**   **|B**   **|**
I've   been   lovin'   you,

Gm   **|C#**   **|**
you've   been   lovin'   me   so

D   **|Dadd9**   **|**
long,   baby nothin's

A/B   **|**   **B** **|**
wrong.   So   I'm   asking,

Chorus 3   **E**   **|A6**   **|**
baby,   baby,   ba - by,

F#m   **B**   **|E**   **|**
(Female) *you   can   have   my   private   num-ber,*

                                    |A6   **|**
Baby,   baby,   ba - by,   *(Male)* You've

F#m   **B**   **|E**   **A/B |**
given   me   your   private   num - ber.

Verse 3   **E**   **|A**   **|**
You know I want, *You know I want,* you know I need, *you know I need,*

F#m7   **Bsus4**   **|E**   **A/B |**
you ba-by.
                     baby, baby, baby,   baby

E   **|A**   **|**
You know I want, *You know I want,* you know I need, *you know I need,*

F#m7   **Bsus4**   **|E**   **A/B |**
you ba-by.

E   **Bm6**   **|A**   **E/G#**   **|**
You know I want, you know I need

F#m7   **A/B**   **|E**   **||**
you ba-by.

Rhythm & Blues Alibi

Words and Music by
PAUL BLACKBURN, THOMAS WILLIAM GRAY, OLIVER JAMES PEACOCK,
IAN THOMAS BALL AND BENJAMIN JOSEPH OTTEWELL

$\quad$ = 66

Verse 1 $\frac{4}{4}$ N.C. |G   C |
You can   write your tunes with rhythm and blues as your a-

D5   **D7**   **G** |
libi.   You can

                    C |
sell your soul   and lay the blame all on the pass-

D5   **D7**   **G** |
ers by.

                    C |
You   shake   your   bo - dy   on   the   T.

D5   **D7** |
V.   screen.   Seems   to me,

Cadd9   **B♭** |
   you   try   anything   twice.

G   **C/G**   **G** |
                              You can

Verse 2   **G**   **C** |
swing it out   and   use it as your   aphrodi-

D5   **D7**   **G** |
iac.   You can

                    C |
give it to me,   to me. Plain to see that I'll give

D⁵   **D⁷**   **G** |
it you back.

                                          C |
    You   let   it   flow,   let   it   go,   there's

D⁵   **D⁷** |
nothing   to   it,   anyone   can,

Cadd9   **B♭** |
          try   anything   twice.

              G   **C/G**   **G**
| /   /   /   / |

Cadd9   **B♭** |
          Try   anything   twice.

              G   **C/G**   **G**
| /   /   /   / |

Chorus 1   **G**   **C** |**F**   **F**sus2 **F**   **Em⁷** |
Chasing after stories that have al   -   ready   been told.

G   **C** |**F**   **F**sus2 **F**   **Em⁷** |
Could not look old Son House in the eye.

G   **C** |**F**   **F**sus2 **F**   **Em⁷** |
I know where you carry such a   fragile   load,   but

G   **F** | **C** |²₄ **B♭** |
I got yours and you got mine. It's a   rhythm and blues   alibi.

Interlude   **G**   **C**   **D⁵**   **D⁷** **G**   **C**   **D⁵**   **D⁷** **G**
⁴₄| /   /   /   / | /   /   /   / | /   /   /   / | /   /   /   / |

                    C   **D⁵**   **D⁷** **G**   **C**   **D⁵**   **D⁷** **G**
| /   /   /   / | /   /   /   / | /   /   /   / | /   /   /   / |

Verse 3   **G**   **C** |
take a trip   through the juke joints smoke filled

D⁵
paradise.   **D⁷**   **G |**
You can

                        C   **|**
give it all   'cause you   are walking a

D⁵   **D⁷**   **G |**
fine,   fine line,   line.

                        C   **|**
You shake your boo - ty   on   the T.

D⁵   **D⁷**   **|**
V. screen.   Seems   to me,

Cadd9   **B♭**   **|**
you   try   anything   twice.

          G   **C/G**   **G**
| /   /   /   /   **|**

Cadd9   **B♭**   **|**
Try   anything   twice.

          G   **C/G**   **G**
| /   /   /   /   **|**

Chorus 2   **G**   **C**   **|F** **Fsus2** **F**   **Em⁷**   **|**
Chasing after stories that have al - ready   been told.

G   **C**   **|F** **Fsus2** **F**   **Em⁷**   **|**
Could not look old Son House in the eye.

G   **C**   **|F** **Fsus2** **F**   **Em⁷**   **|**
I know where you carry such a   fragile   load,   but

G   **F**   **|** **C**   **|$\frac{2}{4}$ B♭**   **|**
I got yours and you got mine. It's a   rhythm and blues   alibi.

Coda   **$\frac{4}{4}$ G**   **C**   **|D⁵**   **D⁷**   **G**   **|**
  (twice)   You   try   anything

                     C   **|D⁵**   **D⁷ G**   **|**
twice.   You   try   anything

(Repeat Coda to fade)

49

Secret Smile

Words and Music by
DAN WILSON

Bbm   Bb   Ebm9   Ab6   Ab   Gbmaj7

Ab13   Gb   Db6   Eb   Dbmaj7

♩ = 96

Intro

| Bbm | Bb | Ebm9 | Bb | Ab6 | Ab | Gbmaj7 | Ab13 |

4/4 | / / / / | / / / / | / / / / | / / / / |

| Bbm | | Ebm9 | | Ab6 | | Gbmaj7 | Ab13 |

| / / / / | / / / / | / / / / | / / / / |

Verse 1

Bbm | Ebm9 |
Nobody knows it, but you've got a secret smile,

Ab6 | Gbmaj7 |
and you use it on-ly for me.

Bbm | Ebm9 |
Nobody knows it, but you've got a secret smile,

Ab6 | Gbmaj7 |
and you use it on-ly for me. So

Bbm | Ebm9 |
use it and prove it. Re-

Ab6 | Gbmaj7 |
move this whirling sadness. I'm

Bbm | Ebm9 |
losing, I'm bluesing, but

Ab6 | Gbmaj7 |
you can save me from madness.

© 1998 & 2000 WB Music Corp and Semidelicious Music, USA
Warner/Chappell Music Ltd, London W6 8BS

50

B♭m		**E♭m⁹**		**A♭⁶**		**G♭maj7**	
/ / / /		/ / / /		/ / / /		/ / / /	

Verse 2

B♭m　　　　　　　　　　| **E♭m⁹**
　　Nobody knows it,　　but you've　　got a secret　　smile,

A♭⁶　　　　　　　　　　| **G♭maj7**
　　　　and you use it　　on-ly　　for me.

B♭m　　　　　　　　　　| **E♭m⁹**
　　Nobody knows it,　　but you've　　got a secret　　smile,

A♭⁶　　　　　　　　　　| **G♭maj7**
　　　　and you use it　　on-ly　　for me.　　So

B♭m　　　　　　　　　　| **E♭m⁹**
save　　　me　　I'm waiting,　　　I'm

A♭⁶　　　　　　　　　　| **G♭maj7**
needing　　hear　me　pleading.　　And

B♭m　　　　　　　　　　| **E♭m⁹**
soothe　　me　　im-prove　　me,　　I'm

A♭⁶　　　　　　　　　　| **G♭maj7**
grieving,　　I'm barely believing　　now,

A♭　　　　　　　　　　| **G♭**
　　now.　　When

Bridge 1

D♭⁶　　　　　　　　　　| **E♭**
　　you are flying　　a-round and around　　the world

A♭　　　　　　　　　　| **D♭maj7**
　　and I'm lying alone - ly,

D♭⁶　　　　　　　　　　| **E♭**
I know there's something　sacred and free,　reserved

A♭　　　　　　　　　　| **D♭maj7**
　　and received by me only.

Verse 3

Bbm | Ebm9 |
    Nobody knows it,   but you've   got a secret   smile,

Ab6 | Gbmaj7 |
      and you use it   on-ly   for me.

Bbm | Ebm9 |
    Nobody knows it,   but you've   got a secret   smile,

Ab6 | Gbmaj7 |
      and you use it   on-ly   for me.   So

Bbm | Ebm9 |
    use   it   and prove   it.   Re-

Ab6 | Gbmaj7 |
    move   this   whirling   sadness.   I'm

Bbm | Ebm9 |
    losing,   I'm bluesing,   but

Ab6 | Gbmaj7 |
    you   can   save me from madness   now,

Ab | Gb |
            now.   When

Bridge 2

Db6 | Eb |
    you are flying   a-round and around   the world

Ab | Dbmaj7 |
       and I'm lying alone - ly,

Db6 | Eb |
    I know there's something   sacred and free,   reserved

Ab | Dbmaj7 |
       and received by me   only.

Db6 | Eb |
    Nobody knows it,   but you've   got a secret   smile,

Ab | Dbmaj7 |
       and you use it   only for me.

D♭6   **| E♭**   **|**

Nobody knows it,   but you've   got a secret   smile,

A♭   **D♭maj7**

| / / / / | / / / / |

Interlude   **B♭m**   **E♭m⁹**   **A♭6**   **G♭maj7**

| / / / / | / / / / | / / / / | / / / / |

B♭m   **E♭m⁹**   **A♭6**   **G♭maj7**

| / / / / | / / / / | / / / / | / / / / |

Coda   **B♭m**   **| E♭m⁹**   **|**

Nobody knows it,   nobody knows it,

A♭6   **| G♭maj7**   **|**

nobody knows it,   but you've   got a secret.

B♭m   **| E♭m⁹**   **|**

Nobody knows it,   nobody knows it,

A♭6   **| G♭maj7**   **|**

nobody knows it,   but you've   got a secret.

B♭m   **| E♭m⁹**   **|**

Nobody knows it,   nobody knows it,

A♭6   **| G♭maj7**   **|**

nobody knows it,   but you've   got a secret.

B♭m   **| E♭m⁹**   **|**

Nobody knows it,   nobody knows it,

A♭6   **| G♭maj7**   **|**

nobody knows it,   but you've   got a secret.

B♭m   **| E♭m⁹**   **‖**

Nobody knows it,   nobody knows it.

Stronger

Words and Music by
GARY BARLOW AND GRAHAM GOULDMAN

[Chord diagrams: Am, G6, Fmaj7, Bm7(b5), E7, G7sus4, G7, Dm/G]

♩ = 124

Intro   4/4   **N.C.** | |
Hey,   stronger,

Am   **G6**   **Fmaj7** | |
                                        so strong,

Bm7(b5)   **E7**   **Am** | |
                                   ah.

Am   **G6**   **Fmaj7** | |
Stronger   every   day.

Bm7(b5)   **E7**   **Am** | |
Stronger   every   night.

Am   **G6**   **Fmaj7** | |
Holding   out   for peace,

Bm7(b5)   **E7**   **Am** | |
now   I'm   feeling   stronger.

Verse 1   **G7sus4** |**G7** |
Watching   as   this   storm   goes   by,

Dm/G |**G7** |
I can   see   the light.   A

G7sus4 |**G7** |
prisoner   of   my   own   design,   . my

Dm/G |**G7** |
hands   are firmly   tied.

G7sus4 |**G7** |
I could just fade away   and

Dm/G |**G7** |
live a life unknown.

G7sus4 |**G7** |
I could be some - where else,   but

Dm/G |**G7**   **E7** |
now I'm heading home,   oh.

Chorus 1   **Am**   **G6**   **Fmaj7** | |
Stronger every day.

Bm7(♭5)   **E7**   **Am** | |
Stronger every night.

Am   **G6**   **Fmaj7** | |
Holding out for peace,

Bm7(♭5)   **E7**   **Am** | |
now I'm feeling stronger.

Verse 2   **G7sus4** |**G7** |
Walking from that shel - tered world with

Dm/G |**G7** |
nowhere left to hide.   My

G7sus4 |**G7** |
naked soul is run - ning free,   my

Dm/G |**G7** |
eyes are open wide.

G7sus4 |**G7** |
Searchin' for the high - er ground to

Dm/G |**G7** |
make my life complete.   It's

G7sus4 |**G7** |
only when you climb that mountain the

Dm/G |**G7**   **E7** |
world is at your feet,   oh.

Chorus 2

Am	G⁶	Fmaj7			

Am   G⁶   Fmaj7 | |
Stronger   every   day.

Bm⁷⁽♭⁵⁾   E⁷   Am | |
Stronger   every   night.

Am   G⁶   Fmaj7 | |
Holding   out   for peace,

Bm⁷⁽♭⁵⁾   E⁷   Am | |
ready   now   to fight,   oh.

Bridge 1

Am   G⁶   Fmaj7 | |
     Life owes me no   –   –   thing,

Bm⁷⁽♭⁵⁾   E⁷   Am | |
I   have   tasted   ev   –   erything.   But

Am   G⁶   Fmaj7 | |
I   can't   wait much   long   –   er,

Bm⁷⁽♭⁵⁾   E⁷ |Fmaj7 |
now   I'm   feeling   strong   –   er.
                       Stronger now,

                  |Em⁷ | |
                                            I'm
     I'm   *stronger*   *now,*   *I'm*

Fmaj7 | |
stronger   ev   –   ery   single   day,
stronger   *ev*   –   *ery*   *single*   *day,*

Am/C |E |
                                oh.

Am   G⁶   Fmaj7 | |
Stronger   *each*   *day.*

Bm⁷⁽♭⁵⁾   E⁷   Am | |
Stronger   *each*   *night.*

             G⁶   Fmaj7 | |
                                 Oh so strong,

Stronger   *each*   *day,*

Bm$^{7(\flat5)}$		E^7		Am				

Bm$^{7(\flat5)}$ E^7 Am | |

babe,   I'm   feeling…

so strong.

Chorus 3

Am   G^6 F^{maj7} | |

Stronger   every   day.

Bm$^{7(\flat5)}$ E^7 Am | |

Stronger   every   night.

Am   G^6 F^{maj7} | |

Holding   out   for peace,

Bm$^{7(\flat5)}$ E^7 Am | |

ready   now to fight,   oh.

Bridge 2

Am   G^6 F^{maj7} | |

Life owes me no   -   -   thing,

Bm$^{7(\flat5)}$ E^7 Am | |

I   have   tasted ev -   erything.   But

Am   G^6 F^{maj7} | |

I   can't   wait much long -   er,

Bm$^{7(\flat5)}$ E^7 | |

now I'm   feeling strong -   er.

Coda

Am   G^6 F^{maj7} | |

Feeling stronger, I'm   feeling   stronger,

Bm$^{7(\flat5)}$ E^7 Am | |

stronger   every   day.

Am   G^6 F^{maj7} | |

Feeling stronger, I'm   feeling   stronger,

Bm$^{7(\flat5)}$ E^7 Am | |

stronger   every   day.

(Repeat Coda to fade)

Summertime Of Our Lives

Words and Music by
PETER CUNNAH, BENJAMIN JAMES ADAMS, CHRISTIAN INGEBRIGSTEN,
PAUL MARATSI AND MARK BRANDON READ

Fmaj7   G   Em7   Am7

♩ = 128

Intro $\frac{4}{4}$ **N.C.** | |
Summertime

| |
of   our   lives,   our   lives.

Fmaj7   **G** |**Em7**   **Am7**
Summertime

Fmaj7   **G** |**Em7**   **Am7** |
of   our   lives,   our   lives.

Verse 1   **Fmaj7**   **G** |**Em7**   **Am7** |
Hey,   girl,   the feeling   is   right.   You gotta

Fmaj7   **G** |**Em7**   **Am7** |
get   out   in   the   sunlight.   *Sunlight.*

Fmaj7   **G** |**Em7**   **Am7** |
Hot   sand,   holding   your hand. You keep the

Fmaj7   **G** |**Em7**   **Am7** |
jammin' in the morning 'til the moon   -   light. We'll have the

Fmaj7   **G** |**Em7**   **Am7** |
time   of our

Fmaj7   **G** |**Em7**   **Am7** |
lives,   in   our   wonder   -   world.

Fmaj7   **G** |**Em7**   **Am7** |
Time   of our

Fmaj7	**G**	**| Em**7	**Am**7	**|**
lives.				Come on!

Chorus 1

Fmaj7	**G**	**| Em**7	**Am**7	**|**
	Summertime			

Fmaj7	**G**	**| Em**7	**Am**7	**|**
of our lives,		our	lives.	

Fmaj7	**G**	**| Em**7	**Am**7	**|**
	Summertime			

Fmaj7	**G**	**| Em**7	**Am**7	**|**
of our lives,		our	lives.	

Verse 2

Fmaj7	**G**	**| Em**7	**Am**7	**|**
Cool	breeze	kissin' the	sea.	I've got a

Fmaj7	**G**	**| Em**7	**Am**7	**|**
sunbeam	shining	on	me.	*On me.*

Fmaj7	**G**	**| Em**7	**Am**7	**|**
Blue	skies,	sea in your	eyes.	Let the

Fmaj7	**G**	**| Em**7	**Am**7	**|**
groove	move my people all a-round		me. We'll have the	

Fmaj7	**G**	**| Em**7	**Am**7	**|**
time				of our

Fmaj7	**G**	**| Em**7	**Am**7	**|**
lives, in our		wonder - world.		

Fmaj7	**G**	**| Em**7	**Am**7	**|**
Time				of our

Fmaj7	**G**	**| Em**7	**Am**7	**|**
lives.				Come on!

Chorus 2

Fmaj7	**G**	**| Em**7	**Am**7	**|**
	Summertime			

Fmaj7	G		Em7	Am7		

Fmaj7   G |Em7   Am7 |
of   our   lives,   our   lives.

Fmaj7   G |Em7   Am7 |
     Summertime

Fmaj7   G |Em7   Am7 |
of   our   lives,   our   lives. *Come On!*

Fmaj7   G |N.C. |
Summertime,   summertime, Sugar candy cherry world.
      Come On!   *Come On!*   *Come On!*

Fmaj7   G |N.C. |
Summertime,   summertime, There's a boy for ev'ry girl.

Fmaj7   G |N.C. |
Summertime,   summertime, Sugar candy cherry world.

Fmaj7   G |N.C. |
Summertime,   summertime.

Interlude

Fmaj7 G   Em7 Am7   Fmaj7 G   Em7 Am7
| / / / / | / / / / | / / / / | / / / / |

Fmaj7 G   Em7 Am7   Fmaj7 G   Em7 Am7
| / / / / | / / / / | / / / / | / / / / |
time   of our

Verse 3

Fmaj7   G |Em7   Am7 |
time   of our

Fmaj7   G |Em7   Am7 |
lives,   in   our   wonder - world.

Fmaj7   G |Em7   Am7 |
Time   of our

Fmaj7   G |Em7   Am7 |
lives.   Come on!

Chorus 3 F^{maj7}   G | Em⁷   Am⁷ |
         Summertime

F^{maj7}   G | Em⁷   Am⁷ |
  of   our   lives,   our   lives.

F^{maj7}   G | Em⁷   Am⁷ |
         Summertime

F^{maj7}   G | Em⁷   Am⁷ |
  of   our   lives,   our   lives.

Coda F^{maj7}   G | Em⁷   Am⁷ |
Baby get ready, get down. Are you up for it? Get down with it.
     Come on!   *Come on!*   *Come on!*

F^{maj7}   G | Em⁷   Am⁷ |
Baby get ready, get down. Are you up for it? Get down. *Come on!*

F^{maj7}   G | Em⁷   Am⁷ |
Baby get ready, get down. Are you up for it? Get down with it.
     Come on!   *Come on!*   *Come on!*

F^{maj7}   G | Em⁷   Am⁷ |
Baby get ready, get down.   *Come on!*

F^{maj7}   G | Em⁷   Am⁷ |
         Summertime

F^{maj7}   G | Em⁷   Am⁷ |
  of   our   lives,   our   lives.

F^{maj7}   G | Em⁷   Am⁷ |
         Summertime

F^{maj7}   G | Em⁷   Am⁷   ‖
  of   our   lives,   our   lives.

She

Words and Music by
CHARLES AZNAVOUR AND HERBERT KRETZMER

Db   Db/F   Gbadd9   Gb   Ab7sus4   Ab7   Edim   Gb/Bb

Bb/D   Gbm6/Bbb   Db/Ab   Gb/Ab   Eb/G   Ab13   A

Eb   D   C#   C#/E#   F#m   B   Ab/C

♩ = 65   Capo at 1st fret

Intro | Db   Db/F | Gbadd9 Gb   Ab7sus4 Ab7

$\frac{4}{4}$ | /   /   /   / | /   /   /   / |

Verse 1   Db |Edim |
She   may be the face I can't for-get,   a trace of pleasure of re-

Gb   Gb/Bb |Db   Bb/D |
gret, may be my treasure or the   price   I have to pay.

Ebm |Gbm6/Bbb |
She may be the song the summer   sings, may be the chill that autumn

Db/Ab   Db/F |Gb   Ab7 |
brings, may be a hundred different things   within the measure of a

Db   Gb   Gb/Ab   Ab7 |
day.

Verse 2   Db |Edim |
She   may be the beauty or the beast,   may be the famine or the

Gb   Gb/Bb |Db   Bb/D |
feast, may turn each day into a   heaven   or a hell.

Ebm | Gbm6/Bbb |
She may be the mirror of my dreams, a smile reflected in a

Db/Ab   Db/F | Gb   Ab7sus4 |
stream, she may not be what she may seem inside   her

Db Gb Gb/Ab Ab13 |
shell.

Intro

| Db   Edim |
| / / / / | / / / / |

| Gb   Gb/Bb Db   Bb/D |
| / / / / | / / / / |

| Ebm   Gbm6/Bbb |
| / / / / | / / / / |

| Db/Ab Db/F   Eb/G Ab7sus4 Ab7 |
| / / / / | / / / / |

| Db |
| / / / / |

Bridge

A |
She   who always seems so happy in a

E |
crowd,   whose eyes can be so private and so

D |
proud,   no-one's allowed to see them

C#   C#/E |
   when they cry.

F#m   B |
She may be the love that cannot hope to

E   C# |
last, may come to me from shadows of the

E♭
past   that I'll remember   till the |

                        A♭/C |
day I die.

Verse 3   **D♭**   **|E^dim** |
           She   may be the reason I sur-vive, the why and wherefore I'm a-

           G♭   **G♭/B♭**   **|D♭**   **B♭/D** |
           live,   the one I'll care for through the rough and ready years.

           E♭m   **|G♭m⁶/B♭♭** |
           Me, I'll take her laughter and her tears, and make them all my souven-

           D♭/A♭   **D♭/F**   **|E♭/G♭**   **A♭⁷** |
           irs,   for where she goes I've got to be,   the meaning of my life is

           G♭   **|D♭/F** |
               she,   she,

           E♭m⁷   **|D♭**   ‖
                     oh,   she.

Printed and bound in Great Britain 3/00